ABOUT FLIGHT

ABOUT FLIGHT

Poems by
Frank X Walker

Accents Publishing • Lexington, Kentucky • 2015

Printed in the United States of America

Accents Publishing
Editor: Katerina Stoykova-Klemer
Cover Photo: Shauna M. Morgan

ISBN: 978-1-936628-36-0
First Edition

accents
publishing

Accents Publishing is an independent press for brilliant voices. For a catalog of current and upcoming titles, please visit us on the Web at

www.accents-publishing.com

CONTENTS

for Moochie and Brenda and us ... always, all ways.

RIGHT BROTHERS

for Cecil

An unexpected tornado
taught us everything

we would ever need
to know about flight

kiting my little brother's
paperdoll body

off the ground
like a black superman.

Tethered to me
with a magic lasso:

mama's instructions
to watch over him.

PARATROOPER

When Brother comes down from a high
he moves like a ghost trapped on the ground
—eyes nervous and searching, thin frame
weathered from the effects of bad habits.

When he stands on the edge   of the porch,
cigarette parked in his lips, coffee cup
cradled in his hand like a loaded gun,
I wonder if he is hunting for his former self,

the one who jumped out of the back of planes
instead of arms. When he ducks his head beneath
a cloud of smoke, I remember how quickly
he turned to roofing after his tour.

Searching for that high became the only
familiar thing he knew, or maybe life
just looked simpler that far off the ground.
When I catch him standing on the edge

of the porch, I wonder if he is staring down
at small towns and cities   or choices
some of them still smoking or simply regretting
the roof   was never quite high   enough.

DON'T CALL HIM ISHMAEL

Hard time didn't make Brother wiser
like it did Etheridge Knight.
He returned home from prison
with a pocket full of excuses, not poems.

You'd thought he'd read Moby Dick
while on lock down, the way he chased
great whites, each encounter separating him
like Ahab from his leg, first from his own
children and eventually from   himself.

Regret is for families forgiving enough
to break their own promises,
not realizing that even if the harpoon
is made of love, it can still drag
the whole boat down with the whale.

We might have understood revenge
and even obsession, but addiction
is more unforgiving than the sea.

JACK IN THE BOX

a non-metal box is being cranked
as a familiar song fills the air
> Round and round the mulberry bush
> The monkey chased the weasel

You follow me to a parking lot, barefooted
humming the tune beneath mock-begging
your puppy-dog eyes, pretend pouting,
and the lie that always opens with
"I promise I'll pay you back this time …"
aren't working so you sing louder
> Round and round the mulberry bush
> The monkey chased the weasel

I've drawn the line at gifts for your children,
food, rent, cleaning supplies, and medical emergencies.
No liquor or drugs   or cash that would become such

You crank up the box again
and use an empty parking space
as your stage
after you eyeball the cigarette money
lounging in the armrest of my car
> Round and round the mulberry bush
> The monkey chased the weasel

I remind myself that you've pissed away
every nickel you had
and that I work so hard for mine,
but somehow all our wallets and hearts
have secret chambers
that pop open when you perform
your song and dance

A penny for a spool of thread,
A penny for a needle
It used to be an innocent children's song
locked in a metal box
but you crank it and us every time
we come close enough to hear you sing
That's the way the money goes,
Pop! goes the weasel

DOMESTICATED

He is methodical and patient
until his hunger kicks in, then
he is relentless, extremely driven,
obstinate and most always successful.

I marvel at his resourcefulness,
his improvisational skills, his ability
to quiet the cold, pain, distance, rules,
locks, family duties and obligations.

I envy that.
I want to be that hungry in search of a poem.

He is an architect of dreams. I am simply
a construction worker with words.

We both get up every day searching for
something to open us up, something dark
and lonely, something worth excavating,
something that might free us both.

He is a self-taught artist, part hyena, coyote
and wolf. I am simply the academy's pet dog.

BREASTS BABIES

Brother graduated from mama's breasts
to a pacifier to his always available left thumb.

When he was only three, we knew
how many steps separated upstairs
from down
by counting the knots on his head
after he reached the bottom.

Ten years later, he traded the end of his hand
for a cigarette,
believing strong coffee and nicotine breakfasts
would change his scrawny limbs into a man's.

He fell in love with Mary Jane in a dark closet
and didn't come out for years.

He was standing on the edge of the roof
when his voice *cracked,* blowing shotguns
with something that had tentacles
ecstatic that he was not afraid of heights.

His preference for the pipe imprisoned him forever
in his boyish frame.

He hoards hard candy, lollipops, popsicles
and toothpicks,
secretly searching for something as satisfying
to suck on as sweet milk.

NOTHING'S PERMANENT

i.

An hour after I land in Tacoma
you say goodbye to a friend
and load all your prized possessions:
one trash bag full of new shoes, a bag full
of party clothes, and an army duffel bag
into the trunk, and we head east towards
Kentucky with only the map in my head.

You sleep through the snow in the Rockies,
our descent into the Great Plains,
two sunsets, one sunrise, and tumbleweeds.

You wake briefly every time I stop for gas
and to smile at the trooper
who pulls me over in South Dakota
for testing the limits of your new car.

Every six or so hours you sit up refreshed,
retell the same story,
drive for forty-five minutes,
then collapse, exhausted.

ii.

Six months later, angry and nervous
'cause they "stole" your car,
you eventually laugh at my sobering question
and admit   you didn't think
they could find you way out here.

iii.

We ran out of bail money, or at least
the motivation to raise it and soon tired
of seeing you between bars, in slices.

I remember the last time we saw you
in an orange jumpsuit, collar up, chest open,
the perm in your hair losing the battle
with its natural self.

I thought you looked like a towel-dried
James Brown, at the end of a four-hour concert.
Mama thought you looked like a scared little boy.

iv.

These days you're not allowed to drive.
You get free rides
to the Emergency Room, family court,
and the county jail
and walk as far as you have to go
to pay off last month's
standby flights
before buying round-trip tickets
with whatever remains.

HE WAS A BAD MUTHA 'HUSH YO MOUTH'

Brother wanted to be like his daddy,
wanted to sing solos on Sundays, wanted to
scream into the microphone,
wanted to make the congregation moan,
urged on by a diamond-studded bishop
who rode around town in a white Cadillac
and hair prettier than James Brown's.

He learned to rooster strut and entertain
down in front of the pulpit,
nicknamed himself "Pretty" and believed it,
had a ring for every finger and a closet full
of neon suits, matching shoes and belts.

In his yearbook photo, he wore Reynolds Wrap
around his front teeth, a tribute to his daddy's gold grin.

He floated into church, draped in costume
jewelry, hair styled in helicopter blades, hovering
so far off the ground, he forgot

it was our mother's funeral.

APRIL FOOLS

i return to the image
of your refrigerator and freezer, again
i want to say it was barren,
devoid of a single morsel of food,
not even leftovers or condiments
saved way past expiration dates.

But what i see when i rewind
is a too-clean, spotless space
staged to elicit a knee-jerk pity response
mixed with a tinge of guilt,
your pretend glee as I urge you
to fill up the shopping cart
and the happy dance you perform
outside of the cigarette shop.

It seems that even when a relationship
has spoiled and begins to collect mold,
if i try to throw away everything
with an odd odor or with hard edges,
distance myself from stale former favorites,
the bread and water of our history together,

there is always nothing left
but a cold, empty box
and my uncontrollable urge to fill it.

BEAUTIFUL ONE

You show off your broken front tooth
when you crack open the front door,
before stumbling off to the bathroom

and eventually back again, wide awake
with your eyes dancing, and pour out a tale
of two women who passed you in the street
and called you beautiful,

two women you are hungry for, even now,
two women you make room for next to you
on the couch as you recount your adventures

sucking in the crisp morning air
that escorts the sunshine through
your dusty blinds and open window,
you stare out at a new day

and not down at the empty liquor bottles
or muddled cups that watched you sleep
from their vantage point just below
the scene of your fondest transgressions

you dismiss the mass of raw sores
gathered Zorro-like around your eyes
and sound out beau-ti-ful and smile,

even if it was a dream, you make us believe
it really happened.

EXPECTANT FATHER MANIFESTO

For Cecil Jr.

Dear Jerome,

I recognize that look in your eye.
All either of us ever got was their names.

And I know it's hard, but I want to tell you
not to hate yours.

Instead   let us love the children we invite
into this world.

Let us give them all the hugs
they deserve and get from them
the ones we may have missed.

Let us be there to watch each first tooth and step,
hear each first laugh and word.
To bear witness, to mark each milestone.

Remember   that our fathers
are who they are,
and we   are only their names,
not their bad habits,
not their wrong choices.

If your child is a son, give him more
than your name.

Give him a life   with you.

YOU HIT LIKE A GIRL

for Brenda,

You always preferred the rough and tumble
over Easy-Bake, Barbie dolls, lace.
When you planned a tea party after school
everybody came to watch you be as ugly as Joe Frazier.

If our small Kentucky town hadn't been so traditional
you would have earned your Golden Gloves
in the ring, with other light heavyweights
instead of doing time in the principal's office

You raised frogs in my biceps with your sharp knuckles,
stole punches to my chest, dared me to cry.
You married a stubborn fool,
a legal excuse to fight in the streets every night.

When I hold you, palms up, through two inches of glass,
your baggy orange jumpsuit framed by institutional gray,
you flinch at my eyes that measure you like fists,
then swing at you in slow motion down my cheeks.

When I deliver the news, your knees buckle.
I lower my hands, stare down at you convulsing
on the floor. The chaplain hovers like a cut man.
All of us wait   for the bell.

TIME IS THINNER THAN GLASS

I had forgotten you were my first kiss
until I see you standing there
behind my sister, waiting   quietly.

Your half smile tells me you remember
too, so I pretend to ignore
the orange jumpsuit swallowing your curves.

In that chasm between my lips
and her ear, I search for words
I haven't found strength to rehearse.

Hand dancing through two inches of glass,
I manage a "mama's gone" and watch her
legs quit—her heaviness fold like paper

into your ready arms. The receiver swings
like a dead man. Time bends. I close my eyes
and kiss you, again. This time it's for real.

CHEST OF DRAWERS

You call it *needing to move furniture*
because you think we are too bookish

or too busy with God to know
that the anxious look in your eye

is as heavy and hard to hold as your hunger,
your appointment with your next high.

I imagine you in a back room behind
a locked door, staring into a flame,

cupping your hands to lift the smoke,
arching your back to rise with it,

hovering just below the ceiling before
sitting your life and us down with a thud,

eyeballing it from across the room before
returning to lift it again and again and again.

MOTHERS' DAY

When the universe reached out for your daughter's
daughter and she reached out for you, your hands
were too full of *furniture* to hold her

after U-hauled the heavy weight in your lungs
from one room to the other and back,
after you cloaked all the nicotine in your veins
in bubble wrap and tucked it away in the brown box

that is your body, you allowed the tattered wings
of family to escort you uptown, where you landed
like the ghost of a woman in baggage claim who
flew non-stop on valium and a glass of wine,

who admitted aloud that she was afraid, of flight,
but not you, who are afraid of nothing, except flying
too low, into a room before the bleeding starts, before
grief gushes prematurely into empty hands,

well after the staff deposits the tiny ink footprints
a dead baby and a pink blanket near her bedside
where a white woman's red roses would have been

HAIKU

Etheridge, your life
has been a road map for us
complete with U turns

Brother poet, your words
continue to instruct us
even from the grave

But I pray that death
is not the only way to
bring my siblings home

WORST-CASE SCENARIO

I open the door to the drug den
where my brothers and sister
have taken their rent, child support,
utility and food money,

promises to Mama
tattooed across my face.

I sing them their favorite lullabies,
forge their names on love letters
addressed to their children,

share one last 'remember when'
and laugh until our stomachs hurt.

I hug and squeeze them as hard as I can,
then usher them all—dealers and users alike,
into the afterlife, with the courage
and conviction of a suicide bomber.

ACKNOWLEDGMENTS

Earlier versions of the following poems previously appeared in the *Cream City Review:* 'Don't Call Him Ishmael,' 'Worst-Case Scenario,' and 'Paratrooper.'

CPSIA information can be obtained
at www.ICGtesting.com
Printed in the USA
LVHW020001180119
604377LV00001B/9/P

9 781936 628360